HEALING IN THE ROOM

A Journey of Faith, Self-Love, and Mental Health

VEE MAYO

This book is a work of personal reflection and storytelling. Any similarities to actual persons or events are unintentional or shared through lived experience.

Published by Vee Mayo

Table of Contents

About the Author

Vee Mayo is a spoken word artist, writer, and storyteller whose words are rooted in faith, healing, and real-life experience. Through her poetry and writing, she creates space for honesty, growth, and transformation.

Her work reflects her journey of self-love, mental healing, and trusting God through every season. Vee Mayo uses her voice to encourage others to embrace their process, find their strength, and walk boldly in their purpose.

Healing in the Room – Introduction

So many times, I have written this book in different versions.
The truth is… this book has been 42 years in the making.

I've tried to tell my story over and over and over again,
but it never seemed to come out right—at least that's what I thought.

I was trying to rehearse my testimony,
trying to make it sound perfect.

But one night, I decided to try again.
This time, I let go of perfection…
and I let God guide me as I told my story.

I once heard a woman of God say,
"What we go through is not for ourselves… but for somebody else."

And that stayed with me.

Over the span of 17 years,
while I was rebuilding my life and working to gain stability,
I stayed with different people.

People were gracious enough to take me in.
And somehow, I was always blessed to have my own room
in someone else's house.

A lot of my healing took place
in a room
in somebody else's house.

That's where the title came from—
Healing in the Room.

I always had somewhere to go
when I needed to get away from the noise.
When I needed stillness.

"Be still, and know that I am God." — Psalms 46:10

A room became my refuge.

It was the place where I prayed.
The place where I read the Word.
The place where I meditated.

It was where I could reset…
renew…
and refresh.

The definition of *room* is:
a space that can be occupied,
a place where something can be done.

The definition of *healing* is:
the process of becoming sound
or healthy again.

So what is a healing room?

A healing room is a place you go
to get away from the noise of the world
and step into the presence of God.

And the truth is—
a healing room can be anywhere.

It can be a bedroom in your house.
It can be a quiet corner.
It can even be your car.

I remember a time when I was staying
at my God family's house,
and I didn't have a room of my own.

So I went outside
and sat in my God sister's car.

That became my room.

That's where I prayed.
That's where I read the Word.
That's where I worshipped.

I did what I had to do
in that season.

Introduction – Healing Reflection

There were so many times I tried to tell my story.
So many versions. So many attempts to get it "right."

But healing didn't come from perfection.
It came from honesty.

I realized that my story was never meant to be rehearsed—it was meant to be released.

Everything I went through… every moment I didn't understand… every time I had to start over… it all had purpose.

And the truth is—my story is not just for me.
It's for someone else who needs to know that healing is possible.

Acknowledgements

First and foremost, I give honor to God,
who has been with me every step of the way.
Thank You for keeping me, covering me,
and allowing me to make it through every season of my life.

To every person who opened their home to me—
thank you.
Thank you for your kindness, your generosity,
and for giving me a place to rest,
a place to breathe,
and a place where my healing could begin.

To those who prayed for me, supported me,
and encouraged me when I didn't have the strength—
I thank you.
You may never fully know the impact you had on my life

To the women and men of God who poured into me,
who spoke life into me,
and reminded me of who I was
even when I forgot—thank you.

And to anyone reading this book,
my prayer is that you find your own healing,
your own space,
your own room.

Because healing is possible.

— **Vee Mayo**

Where It All Began

I was born and raised in Raleigh, North Carolina.
I grew up in Biltmore Hills.

At the time, I didn't realize the significance of the neighborhood I grew up in.
It wasn't until later that I understood—
Biltmore Hills is now considered a historic neighborhood.

Biltmore Hills was developed by John Winters and Ed Richards.
Many Black families began moving there in the 1960s.

My aunt and uncle were among them.
They moved to Biltmore Hills in the 1960s

and stayed in their home until 1998,
when they went into a nursing home.

Eventually, the state took their house
because they could no longer live on their own.

I remember sitting and listening
as they told stories about their life—
how they used to live on Bloodworth Street
before moving to Biltmore Hills.

It was a neighborhood filled with working-class people.
People who raised their children there.

Families who built their lives there.

Many of the children grew up and moved away—
to other cities, to other states—
but they always came back to visit.

And many of the elders stayed in their homes
until they transitioned.

I had a good childhood overall.
But it wasn't without its challenges.

I was raised by my great aunt and uncle,
and they were much older.

They were both born in 1919.
If they were still alive today,
they would be 107 years old.

They came from a completely different generation than I did.
And for a long time,
I felt the disconnect between us.

But looking back now,
I realize—
my aunt did the best she could.

Growing up, the basics were always covered.

There was always food on the table.
There was always a roof over my head.

Every Christmas, I received toys
and the things I wanted.

I never went without.

I may not have had the latest fashions
or name-brand clothes like other people,
but I had what I needed.

My aunt was very strict.
My uncle was the complete opposite—
laid back and gentle.

My uncle would take me to the store up the street
in our neighborhood
and get me simple things—
hot dogs, a candy bar, and a Pepsi.

Those moments meant everything to me.

My aunt didn't believe in a lot of extras,
but she made sure the essentials were there.

And one thing about her—
she could cook.

Fried chicken, macaroni and cheese, and green beans.
To this day,
that is still my favorite meal.

She cooked in those old cast iron pots—
the kind you don't really see anymore.

She was old school.
Through and through.

My aunt and uncle didn't have children of their own,
but they raised other people's children.

At one point, they even raised
my older brother and sister,
although not for a long time.

My siblings are much older than me—
about 13 years older.

I am the youngest of three.

You could say…
I was a surprise.

The way I came into this world
was unique—
and, truthfully,
dysfunctional.

I was not raised by my biological mother,
even though she was in the home.

My mother struggled with severe mental health issues.
I didn't fully understand what she was dealing with at the time,
but I knew it was serious.

My aunt and uncle were responsible for her care—
and for mine.

Growing up,
I didn't know my father.

I would ask questions.
I would wonder about him.

Sometimes I asked my aunt.
Sometimes I asked my mother.

But whenever I asked my mother,
it would upset her.

So I learned to stop asking.

I didn't meet my father
until I was 16 years old.

My brother and sister share the same father.
I have a different father.

But that never changed how I saw us.

They were my siblings—
and that was that.

What mattered to me
was that we shared the same mother.

And in my heart,
that made us one.

Where It All Began – Healing Reflection

I didn't always understand the significance of where I came from. It just felt normal to me.

But looking back, I see that my foundation—though imperfect—shaped me in ways I didn't realize at the time.

There was structure. There was provision.
There was also a disconnect.

And sometimes, both can exist at the same time.

Healing for me came when I stopped judging my beginnings and started understanding them.

How I Was Raised

My aunt was very strict.
My uncle was very laid back.

There were times I would go across the street
to my best friend's house,
or down the street
to my God family's house.

I would ask my uncle for permission,
and he would say yes.

But after a while,
my aunt would open the front door
and stand there…
waiting for me to come home.

She always thought I was doing things
I wasn't supposed to be doing.

Now, I wasn't a perfect child—
but I wasn't doing everything
she thought I was doing either.

Looking back,
I think a lot of that came from her own experiences.
Maybe she had done things
she wasn't supposed to do growing up,
so she assumed
I was doing the same.

The main thing I remember her telling me was:
"Don't bring no babies home."

That was the advice I got
when it came to boys.

And because of that,
I had to learn a lot on my own.

I was naïve…
but I was also protected.

God protected me in ways
I didn't even understand at the time.

I could have gotten myself
into situations
that would have changed my life
for the worse.

But God's divine protection
covered me.

I used to get upset
about how strict my aunt was,
especially when I compared her
to other people's parents.

But their parents were younger.

My situation was different.

My aunt and uncle were both born in 1919.
They were part of what's known
as the Greatest Generation—
people who lived through
the Great Depression
and World War II.

They were shaped by hardship.
By survival.

Their values were different—
personal responsibility,

a strong work ethic,
humility,
and self-sacrifice.

I didn't understand that back then.

But now…
I do.

Now I can look back
and see their perspective.

Even though I didn't appreciate it then,
I appreciate it now.

I was born into dysfunction.

My mother was in the home,
but she did not raise me.

My aunt was responsible for her—
and for me.

My mother struggled with mental illness.
I don't know exactly what she was diagnosed with,
but I knew it was serious.

One of the highlights of my childhood
was Girl Scouts.

I was a Girl Scout
from the age of five
until I was fifteen.

I grew from a Brownie,
to a Junior,
to a Cadet.

I was very close
to my Girl Scout leader.

She played a major role in my life.

I learned so many skills
that I still carry with me today.
And I made real friendships—
the kind that stay with you.

Whenever I had problems with my aunt,
I would run across the street
and talk to my Girl Scout leader.

But sooner or later,
my aunt would be at the window…
looking out,
waiting for me to come home.

So I would go back.

Back then,
it really did take a village.

More than it does now.

And the lessons I learned
stayed with me:

To be honest and fair.
To be kind and helpful.
To be strong and responsible.
To respect myself and others.
To make the world a better place.

And to be a sister
to every girl I met.

How I Was Raised – Healing Reflection

There was a time when I didn't understand why things were the way they were.
Why the strictness?
Why the disconnect?

But with time came perspective.

I realized that the people who raised me were shaped by a completely different world.
Their experiences, their fears, their values—they all showed up in how they raised me.

Healing came when I stopped expecting them to be who I needed…
and accepted them for who they were.

Mother Issues Room

My mother was born in Baltimore, Maryland, in 1947.

Around the age of 20,
she left Baltimore
and came to Raleigh, North Carolina.

By that time,
she had already had my sister and my brother.
They are 13 and 15 years older than me.

And then…
years later,
I came along.

1982.

I'm an '80s baby.

Even though my mother was physically present,
she was not emotionally available.

And as I got older,
I began to understand why.

My mother struggled
with severe mental health issues.

There were times
when it would be 90 degrees outside…
and she would be wearing a heavy coat.

At the time,
I didn't fully understand it.

But I accepted her
for who she was.

And I loved her
for who she was.

She didn't know how to relate to me.

She could only meet me
from where she was mentally and emotionally.

And I understood that—
even if I didn't have the language for it back then.

Looking back now,
I can see how that affected me.

I believe that's one of the reasons
I struggled in relationships.

Because of my mother issues…
because she was emotionally unavailable…

I found myself drawn to men
who were physically present—

but emotionally unavailable.

There's a pattern
when you don't receive something
as a child.

Sometimes,
you go looking for it
in all the wrong places.

I remember when I was 12 years old…

My mother attempted to take her own life.

I was at home,
and I could hear my aunt
talking to her on the phone.

At that time,
my mother had her own place,
not too far from where we lived.

I could hear my aunt
trying to understand
what my mother was saying.

My mother was hallucinating.

She was on medication,
trying to regulate
what was going on in her mind.

After my aunt got off the phone,
we went over to my mother's house.

And what I saw…
I'll never forget.

My mother had stabbed herself
in the chest.

But by the grace of God…
it didn't take her out.

She was rushed to the hospital.

After that,
she was placed in an institution
for about three weeks.

When she got out,
she stayed with us for a while…
and then she went back home.

My mother had a history
of suicidal behavior
and deep depression.

And as a child,
I was trying to process something
that was bigger than me.

Over the years,
we never really had
a close relationship.

It has been about 20 years
since I've seen my mother
face to face.

We used to talk on the phone,
but after she moved
from her last apartment…

I never saw her again.
I never heard from her again.

At this point,
she would be around 77 years old.

And the truth is…

I don't know
if she is still alive
or not.

And that's a hard thing
to sit with.

Not knowing.

I haven't tried to search for her
in recent years.

Because in my heart,
I feel like she chose

not to be found.

So I made a decision.

To move forward.
To live my life.

But I still pray for her.

I pray for her healing.
I pray for her peace.
I pray for her well-being—
wherever she is.

And even in that…

God still provided for me.

Because over the years,
I have been blessed
with mother figures.

Women who poured into me.
Women who covered me.
Women who showed me
what care could look like.

So even though
my biological mother

was not able to be there for me
in the way I needed…

I was never without
a mothering presence.

Because God has a way
of filling in the gaps.

Mother Issues Room – Healing Reflection (Expanded)

There are wounds that don't come from what was done…

But from what was missing.

My mother was present—but not available.

And that created a void I didn't even know how to name at the time.

For years, I tried to fill that void in different ways.

In relationships. In validation. In trying to feel seen.

But healing came when I stopped trying to replace what was missing…

And allowed God to fill that space.

Where Is My Father? Room

Growing up,
I used to wonder about my father.

Where was he?
Who was he?

I asked questions…
but I didn't get answers.

I would ask my mother,
but every time I brought him up,
she would get upset.

So I learned
not to ask her too much.

I would ask my aunt,
and she would tell me small pieces—

how he used to cut grass
in the neighborhood…
little things like that.

But when it came to actually
getting in touch with him…
or meeting him…

nothing ever happened.

No effort was made
for me to know my father.

So I grew up
with questions.

With curiosity.

With a space in my life
that I didn't fully understand.

I didn't meet my father
until I was 16 years old.

That was when I went into foster care
and became a ward of the court
in 1998.

I remember that day clearly.

It was a Monday.

I went to court…
not knowing
that my life was about to change.

No one told me
that I would be meeting my father that day.

So when it happened—
I was caught completely off guard.

I didn't know what to say.
I didn't know what to do.

I just stood there…
looking at him.

The man
I had wondered about
for so many years.

I had heard so many stories
about him.

I knew my mother's version.
I knew my aunt's version.

But in that moment…
I was finally face to face
with his reality.

My father was a quiet man.
A man of few words.

Over time,

I would see him during family visits
when I went back to Raleigh.

And I realized something…

God had answered my prayers.

All those years
I had prayed
to meet my father—

and at 16,
I finally did.

He tried to give me $20
the first time we met.

And I didn't take it.

Because of everything I had heard…
I didn't know how to receive him.

I didn't know how to respond.

But even in that moment…
something had shifted.

Because now,
he was no longer a question.

He was real.

My father passed away in 2011
after battling illness for years.

And during that time,
it was my cousin
who truly showed up for him.

She made sure he was okay.
She kept me informed.
She stayed consistent.

And for that…
I am forever grateful.

May she continue to rest in peace.

She did what others couldn't do—
or wouldn't do.

She was there.

I wish
I could have been there more
for my father.

But at that time,
I was going through my own journey…
trying to find my way.

At his celebration of life,
I remember sharing
how I prayed with him.

I asked him
if he knew the Lord.

That mattered to me.

And deep down,
I knew…

the last time I saw him
in that nursing home
would be the last time.

There were white flowers
covering his casket.

White—
a symbol of purity.

And in my heart,
that's how I saw him.

He wasn't perfect…
but he was pure.

I remember feeling a sadness
that he would never get to enjoy
those flowers.

I had prayed so many times
for him to be healed.

So many days…
so many nights.

But I came to understand something:

My father had a purpose
while he was here on this earth.

And that truth

gave me peace.

It gave me comfort.
It gave me strength.

Looking back now,
I realize—

his absence affected me.

Not because he didn't want to be there…

but because there were barriers

that kept him away.

I was angry with my aunt
for a long time.

For not telling me the full truth.
For not allowing that connection.

But as I grew…
I began to understand.

Some things
weren't meant for me to know
at that time.

Some truths
come later.

I once heard someone say:

There are three sides to every story—
your side,

their side,
and the truth.

There was so much
that happened before I was even born.

So many things
I may never fully understand.

I had questions.
And I still do.

Some of them
have been answered.

Some of them
haven't.

But I am grateful
for what I do know.

And I am grateful
that I got the chance
to meet my father
while he was still here.

Because some people
never get that opportunity.

And even though
he wasn't present in my life
growing up…

I wasn't without
a father figure.

My uncle was there.

He wasn't perfect…
but he was present.

And in his own way,
he showed me
what a man could look like.

And sometimes…
presence matters
more than perfection.

Where Is My Father? Room – Healing Reflection

For years, I had questions.
Questions that didn't have answers.

And when I finally met my father, it didn't erase everything—but it gave me something I needed.

Closure doesn't always come the way we expect.
Sometimes it comes in moments.
Sometimes it comes in understanding.

And sometimes it comes in accepting that we may never know everything.

Rock of My Foundation Room

When I was a little girl,
I already had a foundation of faith.

Even before I fully understood church…
even before I understood religion…
I had a relationship with God.

I talked to God
like He was my friend.

Like someone I could trust.

I didn't know the mechanics of prayer.
I didn't know the "right" way to say things.
I didn't know all the formal words.

But I talked to Him anyway.

And somehow…
He always listened.

At that time,
I didn't know many scriptures.

I knew just a few.

John 3:16—
"For God so loved the world
that He gave His only begotten Son…"

And Psalm 23—
"The Lord is my shepherd, I shall not want."

Those were the only scriptures
I really knew.

But even with that…
I knew God was real.

I believed in Him.
No matter what.

I used to attend church with my aunt
until her health no longer allowed her to go.

And one of the first scriptures
that really stayed with me
was the Lord's Prayer.

I remember it so clearly—

There was a gold plaque
hanging in the living room.

Every day,
I would look at it.

Read it.

Take it in.

Our Father in heaven,
hallowed be Your name…
Your kingdom come,
Your will be done…"

That prayer became familiar to me.
It became a part of my foundation.

I also attended church
with my Girl Scout leader.

She was very instrumental in my life
during that time.

I have such beautiful memories
of going to St. Matthews AME Church
with Mr. and Mrs. Carmichael.

There was always something going on.

Events.
Activities.
Community.

I was involved in YPD—
the Young People's Department.

And Vacation Bible School…

That was one of the highlights
of my childhood.

I also attended Vacation Bible School
at my mother's home church—
Tupper Memorial Baptist Church.

Those memories…
they stayed with me.

Around the age of 16,
my older brother introduced me to Christ
in a deeper way.

That's when things began to shift.

I started attending church with him
at Word of God Fellowship.

And I loved it.

That's where I began to really learn
the Word of God—

and how to apply it
to my life.

Bishop Summerfield
was a man of great faith.

And his wife, Pastor JoNelle,
stood faithfully by his side.

Their lives were an example.

Not just of ministry—
but of marriage.

Of partnership.
Of commitment.

Bishop Summerfield showed me
what a man of God looks like.

Pastor JoNelle showed me
what a woman of God looks like.

And the way they honored family…
the way they talked about
the importance of the family unit…

That stayed with me.

Faith.
Family.
Foundation.

Those seeds were being planted
even when I didn't fully understand it.

I loved reading the Bible
even as a child.

I didn't understand everything I was reading—
but I loved it anyway.

My first Bible
was a children's Bible.

It had stories
from the Old Testament
and the New Testament.

And it had pictures—

pictures that helped bring the Word

to life for me.

One of my favorite stories
was Noah's Ark.

That story stayed with me.

As I got older,
my love for the Word grew.

In high school,
I began reading more on my own.

I had a Teen Devotional Bible—
the New Living Translation.

And for the first time,
I could really understand
what I was reading.

It spoke to me
in a way that made sense.

From there,
I explored other versions—

The New International Version,
The Message Bible…

Each one helped me
understand the Word
on a deeper level.

But if I'm honest…

Back then,
I was more of a hearer of the Word
than a doer.

I listened.
I learned.
I absorbed.

But I didn't always apply it.

I was still in a learning phase.

Still growing.
Still trying to figure things out.

It took time…

But eventually,
I began to shift.

From just hearing the Word—
to living it.

From learning about faith—
to walking in it.

And through it all…

That foundation
that started when I was just a little girl—

never left me.

Because God was always there.

Even when I didn't fully understand Him…
He understood me.

Rock of My Foundation Room – Healing Reflection

Even when everything else felt uncertain…
my faith remained.

I didn't always understand God.
I didn't always know the Word deeply.

But I believed.

And that belief carried me through moments I didn't even realize I was being sustained.

Healing came when my faith became personal—not borrowed from others.

School Days Room

Growing up,
I didn't really like school like that.

I enjoyed learning…
but I didn't like the school setting.

And the truth is—
I didn't get good grades.

Not because I wasn't capable…
but because I didn't apply myself
the way I should have.

The way I could have.

Some of it was lack of interest.
Some of it… was laziness.

But what's interesting is—
outside of school,
I loved to learn.

During the summers,
when I was out of school,
I would watch educational programs.

Shows like
Sesame Street,
The Magic School Bus,
Bill Nye the Science Guy,
Wishbone,
Arthur,
Ghostwriter.

But my favorite…
was *Reading Rainbow.*

I loved that show.

It made learning feel exciting.
It made books come alive.

I used to pretend
I was a teacher.

I would line up my stuffed animals
and my dolls…
create my own classroom…
and teach them.

In my own way,
I loved learning.

Just not the way
it was being taught to me in school.

I was the girl
who wanted to check out more than two books
from the school library.

But there was a limit.

So I went to the local library.

Because there—
I could check out as many books
as I wanted.

And I loved it.

There were times in high school
when I would skip school…

just to go to the library.

I wanted to learn
what I wanted to learn.

On those days,
I would sit and read novels.

I loved fiction.

And I loved learning
about Black history—
the way I wanted to learn it.

Because in school,
Black history was minimal.

It was mostly talked about
during Black History Month…
and that was it.

But I wanted more than that.

So sometimes,
I would pretend to oversleep
and miss the bus.

I would tell my aunt
I was walking to school…

but instead,
I would go somewhere else.

The truth is—
I wasn't just skipping school.

I was escaping.

Because I was getting picked on.

Heavily.

Especially in middle school.

I didn't have friends.

Nobody really talked to me.
Nobody tried to get to know me.

I remember one time,
two bus routes were combined.

And when I got on the bus…

no one would let me sit with them.

I was the only one standing.

I was so embarrassed…

I almost quit school
in the 8th grade.

If I had been allowed to leave,
I probably would have.

I was picked on
for wearing thick glasses.

I had a lazy eye—
which was later corrected in 2001.

I was picked on
for how I looked.

For how I dressed.

For not fitting in.

My aunt had me wearing hairstyles
that were outdated.

Styles from her time.

And I tried to explain to her—

“That’s not what people are wearing.”

In the mid-90s,
the popular styles were buns,
French rolls,
finger waves.

But to her,
those styles meant
I was trying to be grown.

There was a disconnect.

As I was growing up,
it felt like
she didn’t want me to grow up.

She still saw me
as a little girl.

She still saw me
as a little girl.

And at the same time,
she would accuse me
of doing things with boys
that I wasn’t doing.

I believe now…

a lot of that came from her past.

I was also picked on
for not wearing name-brand clothes.

Back then,
it was brands like
FUBU,
Karl Kani,
Tommy Hilfiger,
Sean John.

And I didn't have those things.

But honestly…
I never really cared about name brands.

I cared about comfort.
I cared about what looked nice to me.

A lot of that stuff
was overpriced anyway.

But in school…
that didn't matter.

What mattered
was fitting in.

And I didn't.

When I was in the 7th grade,
my aunt made me get a Jheri curl.

To this day…
I still don't understand why.

I didn't know how to take care of it.

And honestly,
I don't think she did either.

After a while,
my hair started shedding…
coming out.

I had to go to a different beautician.

And she told me

my hair had to be cut.

I knew what that meant.

I begged her
not to cut my hair.

I told her—

"They're going to pick on me at school."

But I didn't have a choice.

She cut it.

And when Monday came…

everything I feared
happened.

I got on the bus,
and immediately—
people started laughing.

"They look like a boy."

I was embarrassed.

But I had to go through it.

Eventually,
my hair grew back.

Then another time,
I got a weave.

And I thought—

"This time… it'll be different."

I got my hair done on Saturday.

But by Monday…

it was the same thing.

People asking—

"Is that your real hair?"

Questions that weren't really questions—
just another way to pick at me.

I never really had the chance
to express myself
the way I wanted.

Because my aunt controlled
how I looked.

Her focus was always the same—

Don't be too grown."

There were days
I sat alone in the lunchroom.

Every day.

No one sat with me.

And I would sit there
and wonder—

“Why doesn’t anybody like me?”

“Why won’t anyone talk to me?”

Those thoughts…

they didn’t just stay in school.

They followed me
into adulthood.

I remember a boy
I had to sit beside
in the 7th grade.

He picked on me
every single day.

He talked about me.
He insulted me.

And I had to sit there
and take it.

I asked to be moved…

but nothing changed.

Then something strange happened.

In the 8th grade,
he started being nicer.

And in high school…

he actually spoke to me.

I couldn't believe it.

But the damage…

was already done.

He may not remember
what he said…

but I do.

I carried those words
for years.

School Days Room – Healing Reflection

Words can stay with you longer than the people who said them.

The things that were spoken to me…
the way I was treated…
it shaped how I saw myself for years.

I didn't feel seen.
I didn't feel accepted.

And that followed me into adulthood.

Healing came when I realized:
What they said about me was never the truth about me

My First Crush Room

Back in high school,
there was this guy…

And in my eyes,
he was the finest guy
in the whole school.

We had actually gone
to middle school together.

And even back then,
I thought he was fine.

Tall.
Dark.
Handsome.

In middle school,
he was quiet.

He didn't really say much.

But when I got to 9th grade,
I became friends with him.

I remember one day

I had skipped school
and went to the library.

And that's when I saw him.

We started talking…

And I couldn't believe it.

In my mind,
I was talking to the finest guy
in my high school.

One thing led to another.

We ended up going
behind the building…

And I did something
I had never done before.

I was only 16 years old.

I had no real experience.
No guidance.
No understanding
of what I should or shouldn't be doing.

And afterward…

I was surprised at myself.

Looking back now,
I realize—

I was focused on the outward.

What I saw.
What I liked physically.

But I wasn't looking

at anything deeper.

Because I didn't know how.

I didn’t know
what standards
I should have had.

Technically,
I wasn’t even allowed to date.

But I still found ways
to interact with boys…

to do what I wanted to do.

My aunt had no idea
what had happened.

I remember one day
I was on the bus…

And he got on.

I immediately tried
to hide in my seat.

I didn’t even know
he was coming for me.

But people on the bus
started telling me—

“He’s here for you.”

And when I got off the bus…

he got off too.

My heart started racing.

All I could think was—

What am I going to tell my aunt?"

We walked to my house together.

And I introduced him to her.

To my surprise…
she was open to meeting him.

She had no idea
what had already happened
between us.

But the truth is…

He wasn't interested in me
for me.

He was interested
in what he could get from me.

What I could do for him.

And I was interested in him
because of how he looked.

At school,
he barely paid attention to me.

He had a girlfriend.

I remember one Valentine's Day…

I went out of my way
to buy him chocolates,
gifts,
all kinds of things.

Thinking…

maybe this would make him like me.

But instead…

he gave everything I bought him
to another girl.

The girl he actually liked.

I was embarrassed.

Hurt.

Confused.

I thought
if I gave more…

if I did more…

if I showed up in certain ways…

he would choose me.

But the truth was…

I didn’t feel like
I was enough.

I didn’t feel pretty enough.
I didn’t feel good enough.

And I believed
what other people had been saying about me.

I didn't know
how to affirm myself.

No one was telling me
I was beautiful.
No one was telling me
I was enough.

My aunt and uncle
did the best they could…

But affirmation
wasn't something
they knew how to give.

So I looked for it
in the wrong places.

And that's where
a pattern started.

Trying to earn love.
Trying to buy affection.

And that pattern…

followed me
into adulthood.

Trying to give more…
do more…
be more…

just to be chosen.

But now I understand—

You can't buy love.

You can't make someone love you.

I remember one time…

I liked him so much
that I walked

all the way from my neighborhood
to his.

It was about an hour walk.

I went to the store,
bought him crab legs…

and walked all the way
to his house
to give them to him.

Thinking…

maybe this would make him
see me differently.

Maybe this would make him
like me.

But the truth is…

He only saw me
as someone he could use.

Not someone
he truly wanted.

And the reality was…

I wasn't even his type.

He preferred dating
a completely different race.

So no matter
what I did…

I was never going to be
what he wanted.

And the reality was…

I wasn't even his type.

He preferred dating
a completely different race.

So no matter
what I did…

I was never going to be
what he wanted.

And that was a hard truth
to accept.

But it was also
a necessary lesson.

Because sometimes…

we try to earn a place
in someone's life
that we were never meant
to fight for.

My First Crush Room – Healing Reflection

I was looking for love…
but I didn't know my worth.

So I gave more than I should have.
Hoping it would make me enough.

But love should never have to be earned through sacrifice of self.

Healing came when I realized:
I don't have to prove m

Foster Care Room

I went into foster care
in June of 1998.

It was shortly after
my aunt and uncle
went into a nursing home.

I remember that day so clearly.

My aunt and uncle
had court that morning.

And I had a youth orientation to attend—
I was preparing to work that summer
as a library assistant.

I even asked
if I should still go.

And I was told…

everything was fine.

But when I came home…

everything had changed.

The house I had lived in
for 16 years…

was padlocked.

I couldn't get inside.
I couldn't get my things.

I couldn't even process
what was happening.

There was no cell phone.
No way to call anyone.

Just me…
standing there…
trying to figure out
what to do next.

Thankfully,
a cousin told me
what was going on.

But still…

there was no plan for me.

No structure in place.
No transition prepared.

So I walked.

I walked around Biltmore Hills…
going from house to house…

telling people my situation.

Trying to find somewhere to go.

But no one
was able to help me.

So I went
to my godmother
and godfather's house.

And thankfully…
they took me in.

My godfather
didn’t believe

my aunt and uncle
were in the nursing home.

He thought
they were coming back.

But I knew…

they weren’t.

I was able
to go back to the house
and get some of my belongings.

And when I saw it…

I couldn’t believe it.

The house was filthy.

Roaches everywhere.

It had become unlivable.

There were so many roaches
they had to bomb the house
multiple times.

That was the home
I had grown up in.

I stayed with my godparents
for about three months.

Then I was placed
in my first foster home
in Raleigh, North Carolina.

It was a hard adjustment.

Because the people
I thought would show up for me—

my brother and his wife at the time…

didn't show up
the way I expected.

I was told
there wasn't a bed for me.

But looking back now…

I see it differently.

Things happened
the way they were supposed to.

Because it was never meant
for me to stay.

God had a greater plan.

I didn't stay long
in my first foster home.

I didn't get along
with my foster mother.

So I was moved
to a temporary youth shelter

for about a week.

Then I got the call.

I was being placed
in a foster home
in Charlotte, North Carolina.

I had never been there before.

And I had mixed emotions.

I was excited…
but I was also sad.

I was excited…
but I was also sad.

Excited
to go somewhere new.

Sad
to leave everything familiar.

But that move…

changed my life.

I arrived in Charlotte
in 1998.

And my foster mother
welcomed me
with open arms.

There were ups and downs.

I was a teenager…
dealing with change,
transition,
and everything in between.

But that family…

became my family.

And to this day…

I am still a part of it.

I don't just call her
my foster mother.

I call her
my mother.

Because she has truly been that to me
since the day I entered her home.

I was in foster care
from the age of 16
to 21.

And I can honestly say…

I was blessed.

Because not everyone
has a good experience.

But I did.

Going back to Raleigh
for family visits…

was always hard.

I would be so happy
to see my God family,
my father,
and my relatives.

But when it was time to leave…

it broke me.

I would get on that train

back to Charlotte…

and cry.

Tears running down my face.

Because I didn't understand
why I had to leave
the place I grew up.

Why I had to leave
what was familiar.

But now…

I understand.

Sometimes…

you have to leave
your hometown

for your purpose
to unfold.

Even Jesus
had to leave His hometown.

He was rejected

in Nazareth.

And sometimes…

what's familiar
can limit you.

God will move you
out of what you know…

to take you
where you're meant to be.

Back then…
I didn't understand it.

But now…

I see it clearly.

I am the woman I am today
because I left.

It was painful.

But it was necessary.

Even now,
I still stay in touch
with both of my social workers.

They were there for me
during one of the most critical times

in my life.

And I get to share with them
the good things
that have happened since.

Not everyone gets
that kind of story.

Some foster youth
fall through the cracks.

Because when they turn 18…

it can feel like
the system says—

“You’re on your own.”

But there are organizations
doing the work.

Organizations that step in
and support foster youth
when they need it most.

I’ve had the opportunity
to support and volunteer with some of them.

Like the **Hope Center at Pullen** in Raleigh…

and **Home4Me** in Charlotte.

These organizations
are making a difference.

Because the reality is…

there is a foster care crisis.

There are thousands of children
in need of homes…

and not enough families
to take them in.

Some children
move from place to place…

carrying their belongings
in trash bags.

Not suitcases.

Trash bags.

And that does something
to a child.

It affects their identity.
Their confidence.
Their sense of stability.

is everything.

And when you don't have it…

you feel it.

Even into adulthood.

I know I did.

But I also know this—

I could have been a statistic.

But I'm not.

I'm a success story.

And I didn't just become that…

I spoke it.

I believed it.

I walked into it.

Because through faith…
through resilience…
through God's plan…

I made it.

Foster Care Room – Healing Reflection

What felt like abandonment…
was actually redirection.

I didn't understand it at the time.
I didn't want to leave what was familiar.

But that transition changed my life.

Healing came when I realized:
God was moving me—even when I didn't understand why.

Foster Care Statistics Room

As I look back over my journey through foster care…
I realize my story is not just my story.

It's part of something bigger.

There are thousands of children
who are walking this same path
right now.

In North Carolina alone,
there are over 10,000 children
in the foster care system.

Some reports show the number
is closer to 10,800 children
in care across the state.

But here's the reality—

There are not enough homes.

There are only around 5,000 to 5,600
licensed foster homes available.

That means…

There are more children
than there are families
to take them in.

Children are waiting.

Some are placed in group homes.
Some are moved from house to house.

And some…

don't have a place to go at all.

In some cases,
children have even had to stay
in office buildings overnight
because there was nowhere else
for them to go.

And that breaks my heart.

Because I know what it feels like

to not know where you're going to stay.

To not have stability.

Across the United States,
there are over 390,000 children
in foster care.

Some estimates say
more than 400,000 children
are in the system nationwide.

Every year,
about 20,000 young people

age out of foster care
without permanent families.

And when they age out…

many are left to figure life out
on their own.

Some face homelessness.
Some struggle to find stability.
Some never get the support
they truly need.

That could have been my story.

it wasn't.

I often think about the children
who are still in the system today.

The ones moving from place to place…
sometimes carrying their belongings
in trash bags.

Not suitcases.

Trash bags.

And that does something

to a child.

It affects how they see themselves.
It affects how they move in the world.
It affects their confidence…
their identity…
their sense of belonging.

Because stability…

is everything.

And when you don't have it…

you feel it
long after childhood is over.

That’s why it’s so important
for people to step up.

To become foster parents.
To support organizations.
To pour into the next generation.

Because every child
deserves a home.

Every child deserves stability.

Every child deserves
to feel loved, seen,
and safe.

And if my story proves anything…

it’s this:

Even in the middle of instability,
God can still create a path.

Even in the middle of uncertainty,
God can still write a success story.

Because I am one.

Call to Action – Foster Care Crisis

If you've read this chapter…
then now you know.

This is not just a system.
This is not just numbers.

These are real children.
Real lives.
Real stories.

Children who are trying to figure out
where they're going to sleep.
Who they can trust.
If someone will stay.

And the truth is—
they shouldn't have to figure it out alone.

So this is my call to you—

Don't look away.

You may not be able to do everything…
but you can do something.

You can become a foster parent.
You can support a foster family.
You can mentor a child.
You can give your time.
You can give your resources.

You can show up.

Because sometimes,
all it takes is one person

to change the direction
of a child's life.

I know…
because someone showed up for me.

And it made all the difference.

There are children right now
carrying their lives in trash bags…
moving from place to place…
trying to hold on to pieces of themselves.

They need stability.
They need consistency.
They need love.

They need you.

And if you can't open your home—
open your heart.

Support organizations
that are doing the work.

Speak up.
Advocate.
Educate others.

Because this crisis is real.

And it's happening
right now.

But together…
we can be part of the solution.

Don't wait.

Don't assume someone else will do it.

Be the difference.

Because every child
deserves a chance.

I Am a Success Story – Healing Reflection

When I look back over my life…

I see every moment differently now.

What felt like confusion…
What felt like rejection…
What felt like loss…

Was all a part of the process.

There were times
I didn't understand what God was doing.

There were times
I questioned everything.

There were times
I felt alone…
misunderstood…
and unseen.

But even in those moments…

God was still working.

Even when I was in a room
by myself…

I wasn't really alone.

Even when doors were closing…

God was redirecting me.

Even when I felt like I was losing…

I was actually being positioned.

I went from instability
to structure.

From confusion
to clarity.

From brokenness
to healing.

And the truth is…

I could have been a statistic.

I could have allowed my past
to define me.

I could have stayed stuck
in everything that happened to me.

But I made a decision—

To heal.

To grow.

To move forward.

Not perfectly…

but intentionally.

And that's what makes me
a success story.

Not because everything was easy.
Not because everything went right.

But because I didn't give up.

Because I chose to keep going
even when it was hard.

Because I chose to believe
that there was more for me
even when I couldn't see it.

Because I trusted God
even when I didn't understand the process.

Healing didn't happen overnight.

It was a process.

A journey.

Layers.

Some days I was strong.
Some days I had to push myself.

Some days I had to sit with my feelings
and work through them.

But through it all…

I kept going.

And now I can say—

I am not who I used to be.

I am stronger.
I am wiser.

I am more aware.

And most importantly…

I am healed in ways
I once prayed for.

I am still growing.
I am still evolving.

But I am no longer broken
in the same way.

And that matters.

Because my story
did not end in what I went through.

My story continued
in how I responded.

And today…

I stand as a testimony.

That no matter where you come from…
no matter what you've been through…

You can heal.

You can grow.

You can become.

And you can be
a success story too.

Nursing Home Room

I remember the day
my aunt and uncle went to court…

and shortly after that,
they went into a nursing home.

They didn't have biological children
of their own.

But they helped raise
other people's children.

Including me.

My aunt had dementia.
My uncle had Alzheimer's.

Looking back,
I believe my aunt
had been dealing with dementia
for years before
she was officially placed
in the nursing home.

She would forget things often.

Simple things.

Like going to the grocery store…
and not remembering
where she parked the car.

I remember my sister telling me
about a time
she went to the store with my aunt.

When they came out…
my aunt couldn't remember
where the car was.

Eventually,
they found it.

But moments like that…

they meant something.

My aunt had been sick
for a long time.

I remember when she was diagnosed
with diabetes in 1992.

At first,
she tried.

She walked.
She focused on her health.

But over time…
she slowed down.

She stopped going out
as much.

Eventually,
the only places she really went
were the grocery store…
and back home.

My uncle…

he wasn't very active either.

At most,
he would go to the store…

and then to the ABC store
in the neighborhood…

and buy a whole case of gin.

He would sit in his chair
most of the day…

watching TV.

And he smoked.

A lot.

I used to beg him
to stop smoking.

But he didn't stop…

until he couldn't anymore.

It wasn't until he went
into the nursing home
that he finally stopped.

My aunt and uncle
were married
for about 60 years.

They loved each other…

in their own way.

I remember how they would fuss.

My aunt would call him names…

and five minutes later…

everything would be normal again.

I never said anything.

I was always told—

“Stay out of grown folks’ business.”

But I watched.

I observed.

And I learned
what love looked like…

even when it wasn’t perfect.

It was hard to see them
leave the home
they had lived in
for over 30 years.

That house…

held their life.

They were among
the first Black families
to move into Biltmore Hills

in the 1960s.

And now…

they had to walk away
from everything they built.

My uncle passed away
in 2004.

I remember getting the call.

But I didn't fully understand
that he had passed…

until the day before the funeral.

I had to scramble
to figure out
how I was going to get there.

I made it
to the train station…

but I didn't have my ID.

So I couldn't get on the train.

I had to call someone
from my church.

They came and picked me up…
and took me to the bus station.

And I made it.

I made it to Raleigh
to honor his life.

But what hurt the most…

was this—

My aunt didn't even know
he had passed.

She wasn't aware
of what was going on.

After the funeral,
when we went back
to the nursing home…

She kept asking for him.

Over and over again.

And there was nothing
I could do
to make her understand.

That was hard.

I used to wonder
what would happen
if one of them passed away.

And then…

it happened.

But I found some peace
in knowing
they were being taken care of.

Because I was only 16.

I didn't have the means
to take care of them.

I was trying
to figure out my own life.

There were no plans in place
for me.

My aunt wasn't prepared
the way she should have been.

And for a long time…

I was upset about that.

But eventually…

I had to forgive her.

Because I realized—

she did the best she could
with what she had.

My aunt outlived
all of her siblings.

She outlived her husband.

She lived a long life.

But in her later years…

she suffered.

There were many days
she didn't feel well.

And I believe
there were things
she carried inside…

hurt…
pain…

that she never spoke about.

My uncle wasn't always faithful
to my aunt.

But they stayed together.

They loved each other
in their own way.

I remember speaking
to my aunt's guardian…

and she told me
that my aunt once tried
to fight the nurses
who were helping my uncle.

And she even called
one of the nurses
by my name.

That stayed with me.

Because it showed me…

how deeply she cared.

She was protective of him.

Even in her condition.

And if there's one thing
I can say about them—

They lived out their vows.

In sickness and in health…
for better or for worse…"

Their love wasn't perfect.

But it was real.

And they did it
their way.

Nursing Home Room – Healing Reflection

Watching people you love change… decline… transition…
it changes you.

There were things I didn't understand then.
Things I had to process later.

Healing came when I chose to forgive, understand, and accept.

Because sometimes… people do the best they can with what they have.

Generational Healing Reflection

As I look back over my life…
and over the lives of my family…

I see more than just memories.

I see patterns.

I see pain.

I see things that were never said…
never addressed…
never healed.

I see generations
doing the best they could…

with what they had.

My aunt…
my mother…
my uncle…

They all carried something.

Things they didn't talk about.
Things they didn't process.
Things they just learned to live with.

And for a long time…

I carried it too.

Not always knowing
where it came from.

But feeling it.

In my emotions.
In my relationships.
In the way I saw myself.

That's the thing
about generational cycles—

You don't have to start it
to carry it.

And if you're not careful…

you'll pass it on
without even realizing it.

But at some point…

someone has to decide—

"It stops with me."

And for me…

that decision
became a part of my healing.

I had to learn
how to unlearn things.

I had to recognize
what was healthy…

and what wasn't.

I had to face

the hard truths.

About my upbringing.
About my experiences.
About the things
that shaped me.

Not to place blame…

but to gain understanding.

Because understanding

brings clarity.

And clarity
creates space for healing.

I realized…

my aunt did the best she could.

My mother did the best she could.

My uncle did the best he could.

And now…

it's my turn.

My turn to choose differently.

My turn to grow.
My turn to heal.

So that what was broken
doesn't continue.

So that what was missing
can be restored.

So that what was silent
can finally be spoken.

Healing is not just personal.

It's generational.

When you heal…

you don't just heal for you.

You heal for the people

who came before you…

and the ones
who will come after you.

You break cycles.

You create new patterns.

You shift the legacy.

And that's not easy.

Because healing requires you

to face things
you would rather avoid.

It requires honesty.
It requires forgiveness.
It requires grace.

Grace for others…
and grace for yourself.

I had to forgive.

Not because everything was okay…

but because I needed
to be free.

I had to let go
of resentment.

Let go of anger.

Let go of the question—

"Why?"

And replace it with—

"What now?"

What do I do with what I've been through?

How do I grow from this?

How do I become better…
and not bitter?

And the answer…

was healing.

Choosing healing.

Every day.

Not just once…
but over and over again.

And because of that choice…

I am no longer bound
by everything that came before me.

I honor my past…

but I am not controlled by it.

I carry the lessons…

but I release the weight.

And now…

I get to build something new.

A new mindset.
A new perspective.
A new legacy.

Because healing…

didn't skip my generation.

It started here.

With me

My Father's Side of the Family Room

I remember the first time
I met someone
from my father's side of the family.

After meeting my father…
the first person I met
was my cousin.

And to this day,
I am so grateful for her.

When I would go on family visits,
she would pick me up…

and take me to see my father.

She kept me informed.
She kept me connected.

She told me about family reunions,
about what was going on,
about the family I had
but didn't grow up with.

Because of her…
I wasn't left in the dark.

I remember going
to my first family reunion
in 1999.

I was excited…
but I was also nervous.

I didn't know
how people would receive me.

All those years
I had wondered
about my father's side of the family…

And now,
I was finally meeting them.

My aunts.
My uncles.

Many of whom
are no longer here today.

But I'm grateful
I had the opportunity
to meet them.

I cherished those reunions.

There was always food—
fish,
hot dogs,
hamburgers,
and everything in between.

But more than the food…

it was the feeling.

Family.

My cousin helped keep
those reunions going.

She carried on the tradition
that my grandmother
had started years before.

I never got the chance
to meet my grandmother.

She passed away in 1998
at the age of 98.

She lived a long life.

And I was told
that she knew about me.

I heard so many stories
about her.

How she loved people.
How she connected with everyone—
young and old.

She was that kind of woman.

And my cousin…

she was close to her.

She took care of her
until she passed.

Over time,
the reunions became less frequent.

Less people came.
Less participation.

But my cousin
did the best she could
to keep it going.

I didn't always get to attend
as much as I wanted to.

Life… work… responsibilities…

But whenever I could…

I showed up.

Because I knew
those moments mattered.

Even now…
I still cherish them.

Things aren't the same
on my father's side of the family.

There are some family members
I still keep in touch with…

and I'm grateful for them.

And then there are others…

who don't reach out,
or never really did.

And I've come to peace with that.

Because I've learned—

Just because someone is blood
doesn't always mean
there's a connection.

And that's okay.

I'm just grateful
I had the opportunity
to meet my father…

and to know
that side of my family.

I remember in 2018…
when my cousin passed away.

She had left something for me.

But when I asked about it…

I wasn't given clear answers.

I had to ask questions.
More than once.

And still…
I felt like things
were being withheld.

So I did something
I never thought I would have to do.

I wrote a legal letter
to another cousin…

asking for information.

I shouldn't have had

to go that route.

But I felt like
they didn't want me
to have what she left for me.

When I began
to question things…

people got defensive.

Upset.

And when I spoke up
about how they were acting…

I told them—

"My cousin would be ashamed."

They didn't like that.

And from that point on…

some relationships shifted.

Some cousins
don't speak to me anymore.

But I had to learn

to let that go.

To release it.

Because again…

blood doesn't always mean
connection.

And sometimes…

you have to choose peace
over trying to hold on
to people

who don't choose you.

I remember in 2023…

one of my favorite aunts—
the last original standing—

passed away.

Earlier that year,
I had already spoken up
about things within the family.

And when she passed…

I wasn't even informed
that she had been in hospice.

There was no communication.

And when it came time
for the funeral…

I was told
I couldn't even ride
with certain family members.

That hurt.

But even in that…

I had peace.

Because in 2020…

I made a decision.

I sent my aunt flowers
while she was still living.

I wanted her to know
I loved her.

I wanted her
to enjoy her flowers
while she could still see them.

So when she passed…

I didn't have regret.

I had peace.

Because I gave her
her flowers
while she was here.

There were many times
I wasn't included
in things on my father's side.

Weddings…
gatherings…

moments I didn't even know
were happening.

And that hurt.

Because sometimes…

you just want to feel included.

You want to feel like
you belong.

But I had to come
to a realization—

I was seeking validation.

And the truth is…

I never needed it

from them.

Because God…

is the one who validates me.

And once I understood that…

everything changed.

My Father's Side of the Family – Healing Reflection

There is something powerful about finally meeting a part of yourself you didn't grow up with.

For so many years, I wondered.
I questioned.
I imagined what that side of my family would be like.

And when I finally met them…
it was a mixture of joy, nervousness, and curiosity.

I was grateful.
Grateful to know them.
Grateful to experience family reunions.
Grateful to hear the stories.

But at the same time…
there were moments where I didn't feel fully included.
Moments where I questioned where I fit.

And that's where the real healing had to take place.

Because sometimes, family doesn't always show up the way we expect them to.
Sometimes there are gaps.
Sometimes there are misunderstandings.
Sometimes there is distance—even when there is blood connection.

I had to come to a place of acceptance.

Acceptance that not every relationship would be close.
Acceptance that not every person would understand me.
Acceptance that I could not force connection where it did not naturally exist.

But I also had to recognize the blessings within that experience.

The cousin who showed up.
The love that was extended.
The memories that were created.

And I learned something very important:

Family is not just about blood—it's about connection, consistency, and love.

Healing came when I stopped seeking validation from people who could not give it…
and started appreciating the ones who did.

Healing came when I realized that I was never missing anything—
I was gaining understanding.

And most importantly, healing came when I gave myself permission to let go of expectations…
and embrace peace.

Young Adulthood Room

Coming into my twenties…

was a very interesting time for me.

I knew
there were so many possibilities.

So many things
I could do with my life.

But I didn't have the confidence
to move forward
the way I could have.

Part of it
was my upbringing.

Part of it
was the dysfunction.

And part of it…

was the lack of affirmation.

There were people
who believed in me.

People who knew
I could do it.

But deep down…

I didn't fully believe it
for myself.

So I struggled
to move forward.

To take action.
To step out.

Especially in my twenties…
and even into my thirties.

I started working
as a cashier at Wendy's.

That was my first job.

It was comfortable.

Familiar.

Something I knew I could do.

And I stayed there
for about 10 years.

But eventually…

I knew
there was more.

I was ready
to move forward.

So I became a custodian
in the school system.

It was a good job.

Good benefits.
Good hours.

Monday through Friday.

Vacation time.
Sick time.

Retirement being taken out.

Stability.

But even with that…

I didn't fully understand
the value of work.

I wasn't naturally
a "work-driven" person.

I worked
because I had to.

Because I needed to.

But deep down…

I always wanted
to be an entrepreneur.

I just didn't know how.

I didn't know
where to start.

At 24 years old…

I bought my first house.

And that was a big moment.

But I lost it

to foreclosure.

Because I wasn't responsible
the way I should have been.

And in 2008…

during the recession…

I made another decision.

I quit my job
in the school system.

Not even realizing

what was happening
in the economy at the time.

I didn't know
there was a recession.

I just knew
I wanted something different.

And that decision…

came with consequences.

It took me about 17 years

to really get to the place
where I needed to be in life.

And if I'm honest…

I could have gotten there sooner.

But fear…

held me back.

Fear of stepping out.
Fear of trying again.
Fear of failing again.

I was afraid
to get my own place again.

Because I didn't know

if I could handle it.

So I stayed
in what felt safe.

Renting rooms.
Living in shared spaces.

Even when those situations
weren't always healthy.

I was surviving…

but not fully living.

And then there were relationships.

I didn't have much experience.

Most of what I learned
about relationships
came from church.

I had a moral foundation.

But I didn't have
practical understanding.

I wasn't really taught
how to date.

How to navigate men.

The advice I received was simple—

"Make sure he's the one."

But what did that really mean?

How do you know?

How do you move?

How do you protect yourself?

Those were things
I had to figure out
on my own.

I was a virgin
until the age of 24.

And when that time came…

I wasn't fully ready.

I remember meeting a guy
at the gym
on the east side of town.

I had just moved
into my place.

He was attractive.

And I wanted something real.

A relationship.

But he wanted something else.

And I convinced myself…

that if I gave him

what he wanted…

Maybe he would give me
what I needed.

But that's not how it works.

That experience…

was not what I imagined.

It wasn't special.

It wasn't meaningful.

Because deep down…

it wasn't something
I truly wanted to do.

I was trying to gain something
through giving something
I wasn't ready to give.

And afterward…

I was left feeling disappointed.

Frustrated.

Because once again…

I was trying to earn something
that should have been given freely.

Love.

Respect.

Connection.

And that moment…

was another lesson.

A hard one.

But a necessary one.

Because I began to realize—

I didn't need
to give parts of myself away
to be chosen.

I didn't need
to prove my worth
to anyone.

I just needed
to learn

how to see my worth
for myself.

And that…

was the beginning
of another level
of healing.

Young Adulthood Room – Healing Reflection

Young adulthood was a time of possibilities…
but it was also a time of uncertainty.

I knew there was more for me.
I knew I was capable of more.

But knowing and believing are two different things.

There were moments where I doubted myself.
Moments where I stayed in what was comfortable instead of stepping into what was possible.

I worked jobs that kept me stable…

but deep down, I knew I was meant for more.

The truth is—I lacked confidence.

Not because I wasn't capable…
but because of everything I had carried from my past.

The rejection.
The lack of affirmation.
The uncertainty about who I was.

All of that showed up in how I made decisions.

I played it safe.
I stayed where I felt secure.
And sometimes… I delayed my own growth.

But life has a way of teaching you lessons you can't ignore.

Losing my home.
Quitting my job without a plan.
Walking through seasons of instability.

At the time, it felt like failure.

But looking back… it was preparation.

I had to learn responsibility.
I had to learn resilience.
I had to learn what it meant to trust God—not just when things were good, but when things didn't make sense.

And then there were relationships…

Trying to figure out love without having a clear example.
Wanting connection but not fully understanding what

healthy connection looked like.

I made decisions based on emotion…
based on desire…
based on wanting to be chosen.

But those experiences taught me something powerful:

I cannot build my life on insecurity and expect stability.

Healing in this season came when I started taking accountability.

Not blaming my past…
but understanding it.

Not judging myself…
but growing from my experiences.

I had to learn that my journey didn’t have to look like anyone else’s.

And even though it took time…
I became stronger, wiser, and more grounded because of it.

Now I can look back and say:

I was not behind.
I was being built.

Transitional Living Room

I lost my home in 2008.

And if I'm honest…

a lot of it came down
to irresponsibility.

I quit my job
with the school system
without having a backup plan.

I thought
it would be easy
to find another job.

But it wasn't.

Not at all.

I didn't even realize
there was a recession
happening at the time.

That in itself…

was a lesson.

A hard one.

And that moment…

marked the beginning
of what would become
17 years
of transitional living.

Looking back now…

I often think—

“If I knew then
what I know now…”

Things might have been different.

I was young.

And I didn’t fully appreciate
what I had.

Being a homeowner
at 24…

was a blessing.

But I didn’t see it that way
at the time.

If I had understood
the value of it…

I would have moved differently.

I would have been more responsible.

But there was so much
I didn’t know.

And life…

became my teacher.

I stayed in many different places.

I stayed with people.

I moved from space to space…

trying to find stability.

Eventually…

I entered transitional housing.

That was a new experience for me.

And it wasn't easy.

But it was necessary.

I was grateful
to have somewhere to go.

Even though
I didn't fully know
what I wanted to do with my life yet…

or how to move toward
permanent housing.

Fear held me back.

I knew
there were things I could do…

but I didn't know
how to do them.

I wanted my own place again.

My own home.

But knowing what you want…

and knowing how to get there…

are two different things.

And I was still learning.

Housing…

is a real issue.

Even now.

Affordable housing
is not as accessible
as it should be.

And for someone like me…

who didn't have a strong family support system…

Transitional housing
became a bridge.

A bridge
from where I was…

to where I was trying to go.

And during that time…

I met some amazing people.

People from all walks of life.

People who were going through
their own journeys.

Just like I was.

Some of them…

have gone on
to do great things.

Some of them
now have their own homes.

And some of those connections…

turned into long-term friendships.

Because there's something about
going through something together…

It creates a bond.

That experience
opened my eyes.

It helped me see beyond
my own situation.

Because I realized…

I wasn't alone.

There were so many people
fighting their way through life…

just like me.

And one person
in particular
stood out to me.

She was an older woman.

And at one time…

she had been wealthy.

She had been married
to a man
who had great wealth.

But after he passed…

her life changed.

And there she was…

in the same transitional space
as me.

I couldn't believe it.

Someone who had once
had so much…

now navigating
a completely different reality.

But what stood out the most…

was her attitude.

Even on her difficult days…

she remained positive.

Graceful.

There was a strength about her.

And she taught me something
without even trying.

She showed me
how to put things
into perspective.

That life can change
in an instant.

That no matter
where you've been…

or what you've had…

Transition…

is a part of life.

And how you respond to it…

matters.

That lesson stayed with me.

Because I realized…

this season of my life…

was not the end.

It was a transition.

A process.

A preparation
for what was next.

Transitional Living Room – Healing Reflection

There is something about transition that will stretch you in ways you never expected.

It's the in-between season.
Not where you used to be…
but not quite where you're going either.

And for me, that season lasted longer than I ever imagined.

I went from having my own home…
to losing it.

From stability…
to uncertainty.

And at the time, it felt like everything had fallen apart

I questioned myself.
I questioned my decisions.
I questioned how I got there.

I knew I had made mistakes.
I knew I could have done things differently.

And for a while… I carried that weight.

The weight of regret.
The weight of "what if."
The weight of knowing I once had something… and lost it.

But transition has a way of teaching you things that stability never could.

It taught me humility.
It taught me resilience.
It taught me how to start over—even when I didn't want

to.

There were moments where I didn't know what my next step was going to be.
Moments where I had to depend on others.
Moments where I had to face parts of myself I had been avoiding.

And that wasn't easy.

But what I didn't realize at the time was this:

Transition was not punishment—it was preparation.

Every place I stayed…
Every person I encountered…
Every uncomfortable situation…

It was all shaping me.

It was teaching me what I needed…
and what I didn't.

It was showing me the importance of stability—not just physically, but mentally and emotionally.

I began to see people from all walks of life.
People who had more than me at one point… and lost it.
People who were trying to rebuild… just like I was.

And it changed my perspective.

I stopped seeing my situation as just my struggle…
and started seeing it as part of a bigger picture.

Healing came when I stopped fighting the season I was in…
and started learning from it.

Healing came when I gave myself grace.

Because the truth is—

Because the truth is—
I was learning.
I was growing.
I was becoming.

Even in the uncertainty.

And now I can say this with confidence:

What I went through did not break me—it built me.

Prayer

God, help me to trust You in the in-between seasons of my life.
Even when I don't understand what's happening, remind me that You are still working.
Give me strength, patience, and peace as I grow through this process.
Help me to see that this season is not the end—but preparation for what's next.
Amen.

Root of Rejection

For many years…

I dealt with rejection.

And not just dealt with it—

I identified with it.

Rejection
became a part of how I saw myself.

It became…

my identity.

So much of what I was dealing with
came from that place.

I felt rejected
by my mother.

Rejected
by my aunt.

Rejected
by friends.

Rejected
by family.

And when rejection shows up
in so many areas of your life…

you start to believe
something is wrong with you.

It took me a long time
to get to the root of it.

To really face it.

To really deal with it.

And to finally…

let it go.

Today, I can honestly say—

I no longer identify
with rejection.

I choose acceptance.

But getting there…

was a journey.

Around 2015,
I was introduced
to the teachings of Derek Prince.

One of my closest friends
shared his teaching with me—

"Rejection: The Cause and the Cure."

I remember sitting
at my friend's house…

listening.

And something
began to shift in me.

The more I listened…

the more I understood.

The more I realized
how deep
rejection had taken root
in my life.

Not long after that…

I came across
a book by John Eckhardt
called *Rejection.*

That book added
another layer
to my understanding.

It confirmed
what I was already learning…

but took me deeper.

And even later…

I revisited the topic again
through *Your Rejection Is Showing*
by Phil Gibson.

Each teaching…

each book…

peeled back another layer.

Because rejection…

is deep.

And it shows up
in different ways.

In your thoughts.
In your relationships.
In how you see yourself.

But one of the greatest things
I learned was this—

Rejection
does not have to be your identity.

And that changed everything.

For the first time…

I didn't just know in my head
that I was accepted by God—

I had a revelation of it.

I began to understand
in my heart…

that I am truly accepted
by God.

And that truth…

set me free.

Because I realized—

The people who rejected me
in middle school…

Did not define me.

They were kids.

They didn't understand
the impact of their words.

And even now…

some of them probably
don't even remember
what they said.

But I do.

And for a long time…

I carried that.

But I had to make a decision—

To let it go.

To release them.

To stop holding on
to people
who didn't choose me.

Because holding on…

was only hurting me.

I remember in middle school…

there was a girl
I wanted to be like.

She was popular.

She was liked.

She had everything
I thought I didn't have.

And I wanted
that kind of acceptance.

Because I didn't have
a strong sense of identity.

So I tried
to become someone else.

But I wasn't her.

I was me.

And at the time…

I didn't know
how to embrace that.

I was a loner then…

and in many ways,
I still am.

But now…

I understand it differently.

I can relate
to the story of Leah
in the Bible.

Leah was the one
who wasn't loved.

While Rachel…

had Jacob's heart.

And for so long…

I felt like Leah.

Trying to earn love.
Trying to be chosen.
Trying to be seen.

But no matter what she did…

Leah still wasn't loved
the way she desired.

Until one day…

her perspective changed.

Instead of trying
to gain love from Jacob…

she turned to God.

And she began
to praise Him.

And that's where
my shift happened.

I realized…

The people who rejected me
in middle school…

Did not define me.

They were kids.

They didn't understand
the impact of their words.

And even now…

some of them probably
don't even remember
what they said.

But I do.

And for a long time…

I carried that.

But I had to make a decision—

To let it go.

To release them.

To stop holding on
to people

who didn't choose me.

Because holding on…

was only hurting me.

I remember in middle school…

there was a girl
I wanted to be like.

She was popular.

She was liked.

She had everything
I thought I didn't have.

And I wanted
that kind of acceptance.

Because I didn't have
a strong sense of identity.

So I tried
to become someone else.

But I wasn't her.

I was me.

And at the time…

I didn't know
how to embrace that.

I was a loner then…

and in many ways,
I still am.

But now…

I understand it differently.

I can relate
to the story of Leah
in the Bible.

Leah was the one
who wasn't loved.

While Rachel…

had Jacob's heart.

And for so long…

I felt like Leah.

Trying to earn love.
Trying to be chosen.
Trying to be seen.

But no matter what she did…

Leah still wasn't loved
the way she desired.

Until one day…

her perspective changed.

Instead of trying
to gain love from Jacob…

she turned to God.

And she began
to praise Him.

And that's where
my shift happened.

I realized…

I had been trying
to fill a void…

with the love of people.

With the attention of men.

With validation
from others.

But that void…

could not be filled
by people.

No matter how much I gave.
No matter how much I tried.

Because it was never
meant to be filled by them.

That void…

could only be filled
by God.

Root of Rejection – Healing Reflection

Rejection became something I identified with.
Not just something I experienced.

And that shaped how I showed up in life.

Healing came when I realized:
I am not what I went through.

I am accepted.

Beware of False Prophets Room

Back in 2015,
when I was living
on the east side of Charlotte…

I went to visit
a good friend's gym.

That's where I met her.

She seemed nice at first.

Approachable.
Spiritual.
Knowledgeable.

She was older—
in her 50s.

Someone I thought
I could learn from.

She talked a lot
about prayer…
about faith…
about God.

And I was drawn to that.

At that time in my life,
I was hungry to grow spiritually.

So when she would call me
to pray at different times—
different watches of the night…

I thought—

"This is good."

I thought
I had found someone
who was serious about prayer
the way I was.

But over time…

something shifted.

She became pushy.
Overbearing.

At first,
I brushed it off.

I told myself—

"That's just her personality."

"She's from New York…"

But it was more than that.

When I had to move…

she offered

to let me stay with her.

But what I didn't know was—

it wasn't even her place.

She had a roommate.

And I had no idea
what I was walking into.

I remember one day…

it was my birthday.

I had just gotten off work
and brought home a cake.

I came inside
and cut myself a piece.

She was on the phone.

And as soon as I cut the cake…

she stopped her conversation

You didn't offer the prophet
any cake?"

I was confused.

I said,
"You were on the phone…
I didn't want to interrupt you."

She told me
I should have interrupted her

because of who she was.

That moment…

showed me something.

She valued her title
more than anything else.

Her identity
was wrapped up
in being a “prophet.”

And I realized—

there was something off.

I even told her…

there is more to life
than a title.

That being a prophet
is just a position—

not your identity.

But she didn’t receive that.

Looking back now…

I believe she came into my life
for a reason.

To show me
who not to be.

And how not to be.

There was another situation…

I was getting ready for work,
about to walk out the door.

And she asked
to use my phone.

I told her—

“I need my phone.
I’m going to work.”

She wasn’t working.

But she got upset.

She started cussing me out…

telling me
I was blocking her opportunities
because I wouldn’t give her my phone.

I felt intimidated.

So I gave it to her.

Even though
I didn’t trust her with it.

I went to work

without a phone…

and she had it all day.

When I came back…

I asked for it.

She told me no.

I had to wait
30 minutes
just to get my own phone back.

And what stood out to me was this—

She would get on the phone
and minister to people.

Give prophetic words.

Sound spiritual.

But as soon as she got off the phone…

She would turn around
and cuss me out.

Treat me poorly.

And I knew…

that was not God.

That was not how
a godly person
treats people.

I remember talking
to one of my godmothers.

And she gave me wisdom.

She told me
what I needed to do

to get out of that situation.

So I did.

I spoke up.
I told the truth
to the person
she was renting from.

And of course…

she didn't like it.

But I had to choose myself.

I had to get out.

Because that environment…

was toxic.

Everyone in that situation…

was dealing with something.

And it was not healthy for me.

I'm grateful
for my godmother's guidance.

Because it helped me
break free.

But even after I left…

I felt hurt.

I felt abandoned.

Because she made it seem like
I was the problem.

She never took accountability.

She spiritualized everything…

but never dealt with the truth.

She tried to isolate me.

She didn't want me
going to church.

She wanted control.

Influence.

Power over me.

She even convinced me
to pay tithes to her—

while she did
whatever she wanted
with the money.

That was manipulation.

That was control.

And I didn't fully see it
at the time.

But now…

I do.

I remember a close friend
telling me—

that she displayed
all the characteristics
of a Jezebel spirit.

Control.
Manipulation.
Domination.

And when I looked at it…

it made sense.

But the deeper truth was this—

I didn't just encounter her
by accident.

There was something in me
that made me vulnerable
to that situation.

I was trying to fill a void.

A void
that came from not having
my biological mother
in the way I needed.

Even though I had
mother figures in my life…

There was still
a part of me
that felt empty.

And I tried to fill that space
with her.

Trying to make her
a "spiritual mother."

But she was never meant
to be that.

And that experience…

taught me something powerful—

Discernment matters.

Not everyone
who sounds spiritual
is sent by God.

Not everyone
who carries a title
has the character
to match it.

And most importantly—

You cannot fill
a God-sized void
with people.

That void…

can only be filled
by God.

Family Matters Room

I have always appreciated
the family dynamic
in my life.

Especially in my early years…

and even into my twenties
and thirties.

Family—
in whatever form it showed up—

meant something to me.

It gave me a sense of connection.
A sense of belonging.

But over time…

that dynamic changed.

It wasn't as strong
or as present
as it once was.

And that was hard
to come to terms with.

But I also realized something—

Family didn't disappear.

It just showed up
in different ways.

Through my God family.

Through my extended foster family.

People who chose me.
People who showed up for me.
People who loved me
without obligation.

And for that…

I am grateful.

Because I learned something
that changed my perspective forever—

Family
does not always mean blood.

One of my favorite scriptures
when it comes to family
is Psalm 133.

"How good and pleasant it is
when God's people

live together in unity…"

That scripture…

represents what family
is supposed to be.

Unity.
Peace.
Connection.

A place where people
come together
and truly support one another.

There is something powerful
about being around
a unified family.

You can feel it.

There’s peace there.
There’s love there.
There’s safety there.

And I believe—

that’s how it’s supposed to be.

But the truth is…

not every family
operates that way.

Some families…

are broken.

Some are disconnected.

Some are unhealthy.

Some are toxic.

And that’s a reality
many people have to face.

Including me.

My family dynamic
was not perfect.

But I am still thankful
for what I did have.

What About Your Friends? Room

Growing up…

I didn't really understand
the value of friendship.

Not the way I do now.

If I'm honest…

I wasn't what you would call
a good friend.

And a lot of that came from
not knowing who I was.

Not being confident
in who I was.

I was a loner.

I spent a lot of time
by myself.

As a little girl,
I mostly played alone.

I did have one friend
who lived across the street.

She was about three years
younger than me.

And she was one of my best friends
growing up.

But when I moved
to Charlotte…

Things changed.

The friendship
was never the same.

I saw her again
years later

when I moved back to Raleigh
for a short time in 2011…

But by then…

we had both grown.

And sometimes…

growth changes relationships.

People change.

Friendships change.

I used to wonder
why I didn't have
a lot of friends growing up.

Especially in school.

In middle school…

I had no friends.

I was picked on
every single day.

Nobody talked to me.

Nobody really liked me.

And that affected me
more than I realized
at the time.

Things got a little better
in high school.

I had one or two people
I could talk to.

There was one girl
who was a good friend to me.

But I didn't fully appreciate
that friendship.

Because I was so caught up
in what I was dealing with
internally.

The hurt.

The rejection.

The things people had said about me.

I carried all of that

into my friendships.

There's a saying—

"Hurt people hurt people."

And in some ways…

that was me.

Not always intentionally…

but it showed up.

In how I connected.
In how I responded.

In how I showed up.

I had to learn…

what it really meant
to be a friend.

Not just having friends—

but being one.

And that took time.

It took growth.

It took healing.

Now…

I'm intentional.

I make an effort
to show up for the people
in my life.

The ones I call friends…

and the ones
who call me a friend.

I don't want

to let people down.

Even when my schedule
doesn't always allow me
to be physically present…

I still show up
in other ways.

I support them.

I celebrate them.

I reach out.

I encourage them.

A message.
A post.
A simple "I'm proud of you."

It all matters.

And I do it
to the best of my ability.

Because I understand now…

friendship requires effort.

There have been times
when I wish
I could have done more.

Times when I felt like
I didn’t show up
the way I wanted to.

But I’ve learned
to give myself grace.

Love and Forgiveness Room

I used to think
love and forgiveness
were two separate things.

But one day…

a friend of mine
helped me see differently.

A spiritual brother
said something to me
that stayed with me—

Love and forgiveness
go together.

They are not separate.

They are one
and the same.

And that shifted
my understanding.

Because I had to learn…

how to forgive.

Not just the easy things.

But the hard things.

The people who hurt me.

The people who abandoned me.
The people who rejected me.
The people who mistreated me.
The people who overlooked me.
The people who only tolerated me.

Forgiveness…

was not easy.

And I realized something—

Forgiveness
is not a one-time decision.

It's a process.

A daily decision.

A moment-by-moment choice.

Because sometimes…

you forgive someone…

And then the memory
comes back.

And you have to choose
to forgive again.

That's when I understood
what the scripture meant—

"Forgive seventy times seven."

—Matthew 18:21–22

That wasn't about a number.

That was about a posture.

A lifestyle.

Forgiveness
is not based on feelings.

Because if I went
based on how I felt…

There are people
I would have never forgiven.

But forgiveness
is a decision.

A choice
to release.

To let go.

To not hold it
against them anymore.

And sometimes…

that choice
is for you.

There have been times
when I had to go to people…

And apologize.

To take responsibility
for what I said…
for what I did.

And there were times
when people came to me…

And asked
for my forgiveness.

And I gave it.

Not because
it didn't hurt.

But because
I chose freedom.

Because unforgiveness…

keeps you bound.

I remember
about 10 years ago…

my god sister
came to me.

And she asked me

to forgive her
for how she treated me.

And I did.

But not only that…

I asked her
to forgive me.

For anything

I had said or done
that wasn't right.

We made peace.

We made things right.

And I'm so grateful
that we did.

Because today…

she is no longer here.

She transitioned in 2024.

And even though
I was saddened by her passing…

I had peace.

Because there was
nothing left unresolved.

. No guilt.

No regret.

We had already
made amends.

And that…

is priceless.

She taught me so much
about love
and forgiveness.

She didn't just talk about it…

She lived it.

She was an example.

And her life
reminded me—

Don't hold on
to things too long.

Don't wait.

Make it right
while you can.

Because tomorrow
is not promised.

Love and forgiveness…

go together.

You can't say you love
and not forgive.

And you can't truly forgive…

without love.

They are connected.

They are one.

And I've learned—

Unforgiveness
is unhealthy.

It weighs you down.
It affects your mind.
It affects your body.
It affects your spirit.

It keeps you stuck.

But forgiveness…

frees you.

It allows you
to move forward.

The Best Cousin Room

I am so thankful
and so grateful
for my dear cousin.

May she continue
to rest in peace.

I remember the first time
I met her…

back in 1998.

That was when I became
a ward of the court
and entered foster care.

She was one of the first people
on my father's side of the family
that I met…

after meeting my father.

And from the beginning…

there was something different
about her.

She was one of a kind.

There was no one else
like her in the family.

She was the one
who held everything together.

She organized
the family reunions.

She kept the traditions alive…

especially after my grandmother,
Grandma Maggie.

And when she passed…

things were never the same.

It took me a long time
to accept that.

To accept
that things would never go back
to how they were
when she was here.

And through that…

I began to see people
for who they really were.

She had told me
back in 2016
about some things
she wanted to leave for me.

I didn’t think much of it
at the time.

I didn’t know…

that just two years later…

she would be gone.

I remember the day
I found out she passed.

I was at work.

But that morning…

something didn't feel right.

I couldn't explain it.

And I tried to ignore it…

because I had just come off
a beautiful birthday weekend.

There was no reason
for me to feel that way.

But something
in my spirit…

knew.

Later that day,
while I was at work…

my cousin reached out to me
on Facebook Messenger.

He told me
to call him.

But I couldn't.

I was working
at the airport at the time,
at a checkpoint.

And as soon as I saw
that message…

everything shifted.

I knew.

I told my coworker
I needed to go
to the bathroom.

And I cried.

For 45 minutes.

Because I could not believe…

she was gone.

Somehow…

I pulled myself together
and finished my shift.

I didn't go home…

because I had already taken time off
and didn't want to miss work.

But my heart…

was heavy.

It was a shock
to everyone.

Her sisters—
my other cousins—

were devastated.

The cousin who messaged me…

he was the one
who had to tell everyone.

He was listed
as her emergency contact.

I later learned
that her job
had done a welfare check.

They had to get permission
to enter her home.

And that's when
she was found…

no longer here.

I often think about that moment.

A regular day.

A Monday morning.

Getting ready for work…

like she always did.

And then…

And then…

just like that.

Gone.

She was so close
to retirement.

And I remember thinking…

how unfair it felt.

That she didn't get to enjoy
the fruits of her labor.

After everything she had done.

After everything
she had given.

She had already faced
health challenges.

After her stroke in 2012…

she became more aware
of her health.

And I remember
being there for her
during that time.

I stayed with her
after she got out
of the hospital.

And that was an honor.

I'm so grateful
I was in Raleigh
at that time
to be able to do that.

Because she had always
been there for others.

For her aunts.
For her uncles.
For the family.

And in that moment…

I was able
to be there for her.

That means everything to me.

I hold on
to those memories.

The visits to Raleigh…

I hold on
to those memories.

The visits to Raleigh…

when she would make sure
I got to see my father.

The road trips
to Norfolk, Virginia…

to visit one of my favorite aunts.

I remember the first time
going through
the underwater tunnel.

I kept looking up…

thinking I would see water
above us.

I was so amazed.

And she went to Norfolk
every single year…

Until the year
she passed.

That was the only year
she didn't go.

She carried herself
with class.

She dressed well.

Always.

I never saw her
in a pair of jeans.

She represented herself
with dignity.

And she gave so much
to all of us.

She was truly
an angel on earth.

And now…

she’s an angel in heaven.

And even though
she’s no longer here…

Her impact…

still lives on.

Friends Behind the Wall Room

Back in 2014…

I started something
out of curiosity.

It all began
when I went looking
for my first crush—

a guy I went to high school with.

I found out
he had been locked up
in South Carolina…

but had gotten out.

And that made me wonder—

What would it be like
to write someone
who is currently incarcerated?

At first…

it was innocent.

I just wanted
to encourage someone.

To reach out
to brothers behind the wall…

say a few uplifting words…

and move on.

So I went on
a site called *Meet-An-Inmate…*

and I found a few people
to write.

That's how it started.

The first guy I wrote
was in New York.

And from the beginning…

he said all the right things.

Everything
I wanted to hear.

And I believed it.

I took it in…

word for word.

I didn't ask
enough questions
about his past.

And when I finally did…

something changed.

He became distant.

Different.

Months later,
I wrote him again…

thinking I was responding
to feelings
he had already expressed.

But then he told me—

he only saw me

as a friend.

And I was confused.

Because that's not
what those letters said.

To this day…

I believe
someone else
may have been writing
those letters.

Because it didn't match.

But at the time…

I didn't question it enough.

Because I wanted
to believe it was real.

During that season…

I didn't have much going on.

I was working
at Food Lion…

coming home…

and writing letters.

Long letters.

Sometimes five pages…

once a week.

Writing became my outlet.

But it also opened the door

for manipulation.

Because words…

can create an illusion.

And I was caught
in that illusion.

Then there was another man
I wrote to in Ohio.

He was incarcerated
for crimes he had committed…

and eventually,
he was released.

When he got out…

I reached out to him
on Facebook.

We exchanged numbers…

and I called him.

But the way he responded to me
in the free world…

was completely different.

When he was locked up…

he said everything
I wanted to hear.

But when he was free…

his actions
didn't match his words.

And that showed me something.

A lot of times…

people will say
what sounds good

in one environment…

But live differently
in another.

Then there was a third man…

someone I wrote to
off and on
starting in 2014.

He was incarcerated
in Kentucky.

He had been locked up
for about 12 years.

I wrote him
for about three years…

then stopped.

And then
I started writing him again
in 2020.

He told me
he was eligible for parole
in 2022.

And in my mind…

something shifted.

I started thinking—

"I need to be the one for him."

"I need to show him
I'm a good woman."

He told me
he had been married before…

but that his wife
stopped doing
what he wanted
after they got married.

And somehow…

I internalized that.

I felt like
I had to prove myself.

To someone
I had never even met
in real life.

Looking back now…

I see it clearly.

That was low self-esteem.

That was a need
for validation.

That was trying
to earn something
that should be given freely.

And the truth is…

All three of those men…

were likely writing
other women too.

Deep down…

I knew that.

But I ignored it.

Because I wanted
to feel chosen.

But here's the reality—

Not one of them
reached out to me

once they were free.

Not one.

And at first…

that could have been
disappointing.

But now…

I see it differently.

I'm actually happy
for them.

Because they are free.

They have the opportunity
to live their lives.

And that's a blessing.

But for me…

It was a lesson.

A powerful one.

Because what I realized is—

Even though
I was in the free world…

I wasn't free.

Not mentally.
Not emotionally.
Not spiritually.

I was searching.

Trying to fill a void.

Trying to feel seen.

Trying to feel chosen.

And that experience…

was a mirror.

It showed me
where I was.

And what I needed
to heal.

Because there are people…

walking around free…

But still bound.

Bound in their thinking.
Bound in their emotions.
Bound in their spirit.

And I was one of them.

But that season…

helped me see it.

And once you see it…

you can begin to change it.

Because true freedom…

Is not just being free physically.

It's being free
in your mind…
your heart…
and your spirit.

And that's the kind of freedom
I began to pursue.

Mental Breakdown Crisis Room

In 2014…

I experienced
a mental breakdown.

At the time,
I was renting a room.

Even though
the rent was only $300 a month…

It was still a struggle.

I was working
at Food Lion…

and making just enough
to survive.

To pay rent.
To get back and forth to work.

And I was receiving food stamps.

But even with that…

I was barely making it.

There were days
I ate every other day.

That was my reality.

And it was stressful.

It felt like
everything was piling up
at once.

I was doing my best…

but it didn't feel like enough.

I would pray…

and pray…
and pray…

But it felt like
nothing was changing.

Like I was stuck.

Like my life
was at a standstill.

I applied for jobs…

but didn't get them.

I didn't have much experience.

And it felt like
doors just wouldn't open.

At the same time…

I was caught up
in something else.

An illusion.

I was writing someone
in New York…

believing
we had a relationship.

But we didn't.

It wasn't real.

It was something
I held on to…

because I didn't have
anything else.

All my time…

all my energy…

was invested
in something
that wasn't even real.

And it became overwhelming.

Everything did.

And then one day…

I had my first
major anxiety attack.

I was at home…

by myself.

And I had never
felt anything like it before.

My heart was racing.

I was hyperventilating.

I was scared.

I thought
I was dying.

I didn't know

what was happening.

It took me 10 minutes
just to call 911.

That's how afraid I was.

When the ambulance came…

they gave me something
to calm me down.

They also gave me
anxiety medication.

But for me…

it made me feel worse.

More anxious.

And that was just
the beginning.

I had more anxiety attacks
after that.

I became afraid
of the morning.

Afraid of the night.

That anxious feeling
would come…

and I didn't know
how to stop it.

I was even afraid
to ride the bus.

I remember one day…

I was out…

and I felt overwhelmed.

The anxiety hit me again.

And I called
mobile crisis.

They sent the police
to pick me up…

and take me
to a mental health emergency center.

Later that night…

I was able to go home.

But that season…

affected everything.

My job.
My living situation.
My stability.

I almost lost my job
at Food Lion…

because of what I was dealing with.

But by the grace of God…

I made it through.

I used my resources.

I advocated for myself.

And I leaned
on the people around me.

I remember being
at a friend's house…

and they prayed for me.

I will never forget that.

Because in that moment…

I needed prayer.

I needed covering.

And I'm so grateful
for the people
who stood in the gap for me.

During that time…

I prayed like never before.

I would play the Bible
on my computer…

all night long.

From the time I went to sleep
to the time I woke up.

I needed peace.

I needed something
to calm my mind.

I also talked
to a counselor
for a short period of time.

And that helped.

It gave me a space
to process…

what I was feeling.

The fear.
The anxiety.
The confusion.

And I learned something important—

Depression is real.

Anxiety is real.

These are not things
to ignore.

These are not things
to hide.

They are real experiences…

that many people go through.

I've dealt with depression
at different points in my life.

In high school.

In 2013–2014.

And again
in 2023 and 2024…

while dealing with grief.

That grief…

was heavy.

I lost people
I was close to.

And it affected me deeply.

During that time…

I was what you would call
functioning.

I went to work every day.

I showed up.

I performed well.

I even received recognition
and accolades.

But on the inside…

I was hurting.

I was smiling
on the outside…

but crying
on the inside.

If I had the option…

I would have stayed in bed.

But I couldn't.

I had to keep going.

I did everything
I knew to do.

I prayed.
I worshiped.
I read the Word.
I fasted.

But in that season…

it didn't feel like
it was enough.

I made a personal decision
not to take medication.

That was my choice.

For others…

medication may be necessary.

And that's okay.

But for me…

I wanted to approach it
holistically.

And it took time.

But I came through it.

I used the free counseling sessions
offered through my job.

And that helped me
process grief…

and even my thoughts
about death.

Because that was something
I struggled with deeply.

I also joined
a grief support group.

I wasn't able to stay long
because of my schedule…

But it's something
I plan to return to.

Because healing…

is ongoing.

And if there's one thing
I've learned…

it's this—

If you are dealing
with anxiety or depression…

Talk to someone.

Someone you trust.

Because not everyone
will understand.

And not everyone
will have the right words.

But the right person…

can make a difference.

And if you don't have
someone you can talk to…

Talk to a professional.

Because help is available.

You don't have to suffer
in silence.

And most importantly…

You don't have to go through it
alone.

Mental Breakdown Crisis Room – Healing Reflection

There was a moment when everything felt like too much.

I didn't understand what was happening to me.
The anxiety. The fear. The overwhelm.

But I made it through.

Healing came when I allowed myself to get help, to talk, to process.

Resources – Mental Health Support

If you are reading this
and you find yourself
in a place of anxiety, depression, or emotional overwhelm…

Please know this—

You are not alone.

And there is help available.

Sometimes the strongest thing you can do
is reach out.

Immediate Help (Crisis Support)

If you are in immediate distress
or feel like you may harm yourself…

- Call or text **988 Suicide & Crisis Lifeline**
  (Available 24/7, free and confidential)
- You can also dial **911**
  or go to your nearest emergency room

Mental Health Support

- **National Alliance on Mental Illness (NAMI)**
  Offers education, support groups, and resources
  Website: nami.org
- **Substance Abuse and Mental Health Services Administration**
  Treatment locator and mental health resources
  Website: samhsa.gov

Counseling & Therapy Options

- Check with your job for **Employee Assistance Programs (EAP)**
  (Many offer free counseling sessions)
- Local community mental health centers
  (Often offer low-cost or sliding scale services)
- Faith-based counseling (if aligned with your beliefs)

Grief Support

- **GriefShare**
  Support groups for those dealing with loss
  Website: griefshare.org

Practical Support Tips

- Talk to someone you trust
- Write your thoughts out
- Spend time in prayer, meditation, or stillness
- Give yourself grace—healing takes time
- Take it one day at a time

A Final Reminder

There is no shame
in needing help.

There is no weakness
in talking to someone.

And there is no timeline
on healing.

You are worthy
of peace.

You are worthy
of healing.

And you are worthy
of being here.

Real Relationship with God Room

Over the years…

I have come to understand
what it truly means…

to have a real relationship
with God.

Not just what I was taught.

Not just what I heard.

But what I experienced
for myself.

I remember around 2017…

I began to awaken spiritually.

Something in me
started to question…

"Is there more?"

More than what I was hearing.
More than what was being taught.
More than what I was experiencing in church.

And the answer was—

Yes.

Now don't get me wrong…

What I learned in church
had its place.

It gave me a foundation.

But I realized…

There was more to the story
than what was being presented.

There were things
I needed to discover
for myself.

And I couldn't stay
at the surface level anymore.

Because what good
is a foundation…

If you never build
the house?

For a long time…

I depended on other people.

To pray for me.
To encourage me.

To give me a word.
To tell me what God was saying.

And there's nothing wrong
with that…

But I wasn't taught
how to tap into God
for myself.

So I relied on pastors.

On leaders.
On friends
who I thought were stronger
than me spiritually.

But then…

everything changed.

In 2019…

I stepped into a deeper
spiritual journey.

And then in 2020…

the pandemic came.

And the world shifted.

Churches closed.

And for many people…

that felt like a loss.

But for me…

It was a turning point.

Because it forced me
to go within.

I had already stopped
attending church in 2019…

Partly because
I didn't feel like I fit in.

But I never lost
my relationship with God.

And during the pandemic…

That relationship
grew stronger
than ever before.

I began to read the Bible
like never before.

I studied the Word
for myself.

Not just hearing it…

but seeking to understand it.

I prayed more.

I worshiped at home.

I listened to sermons online.

And something amazing happened—

I grew more
during that time…

Than I had
in the previous 20 years
of attending church.

Not to take away
from the leaders
who poured into me…

Because I learned a lot
from them.

But I had to get to a place…

where I knew God
for myself.

Where my faith
was my own.

Where I wasn't dependent
on someone else's relationship
with God…

To sustain mine.

There were times…

when I wanted to reach out
to certain people…

People who used to pray for me.
Encourage me.
Speak into my life.

But they were no longer here.

They had transitioned.

And in those moments…

I had to sit with that reality.

I couldn't call them.

I couldn't reach them.

But I could remember
what they taught me.

I could hold on
to the wisdom
they left behind.

And most importantly…

I could go to God
for myself.

That changed everything.

My spiritual awakening
started in 2019…

But it deepened
in 2020.

That was the season
where my faith
became real.

Personal.

Not borrowed.

Not dependent.

But mine.

And I'm still grateful
for the people
I can talk to…

The ones
who support me.

But I also understand now…

Everyone is going through
their own journey.

And sometimes…

they may not always be available.

And that's okay.

Because I have learned—

My relationship with God
is the most important relationship

I will ever have.

More than friendships.

More than connections.

Because everything else…

can change.

But God…

remains.

And when you learn

how to truly connect with Him…

You realize—

You were never alone.

Real Relationship with God Room – Healing Reflection

I had to learn God for myself.

Not through others.
Not through religion alone.

But through relationship.

Healing came when I stopped depending on others to hear God for me…
and started seeking Him for myself.

Self Love and Self Care Room

Back in 2017…

I began a journey
that would change my life—

A journey
of self-love
and self-care.

Before that…

I didn't really understand
what it meant
to love myself.

I was always looking
for love from other people.

Hoping that
if they loved me…

I would finally feel
good about myself.

But that wasn't working.

And that's when
I came across
Andrea Lewis on YouTube.

She talked a lot
about self-love
and self-care.

And something
about her message…

resonated with me.

It was new to me.

But it was also
exactly what I needed.

Then I started listening to
Tonya TKO.

And I learned
even more.

One of the videos
that truly changed things for me
was—

"How to Love Yourself / Self Love Even When You Hate Yourself."

That video…

was eye-opening.

It was the beginning
of my self-love journey.

I could relate
to her story.

The insecurities.
The impact of what people say.
The way it shapes
how you see yourself.

And one of the biggest things
I took from that video
was this—

Acknowledge
your imperfections.

Don't run from them.

Don't hide them.

Face them.

I had to be honest
with myself.

There were things
I didn't like about my body.

I didn't like being
more bottom-heavy
than top-heavy.

I was insecure
about my stomach.

I thought it was just belly fat…

But later,
I realized…

It was connected
to endometriosis.

What they call
an "endo belly."

And for so long…

I was trying

to fix something
without understanding
what it really was.

I was focused
on losing weight…

Trying to look
a certain way.

But my focus was wrong.

So I shifted.

Instead of trying
to be "skinny"…

I started focusing
on being healthy.

And that changed everything.

I began to embrace
my body.

My shape.

My uniqueness.

Because I realized—

Beauty is not one standard.

I used to think
beauty looked like
Beyoncé,

Janet Jackson,
or Halle Berry.

But the truth is—

Everyone
is beautiful
in their own way.

Society has a standard…

But that's not
the only standard.

Another thing
that changed my life
was learning
about self-talk.

Before that…

I didn't even know
what self-talk was.

But once I became aware…

I realized
how much negative self-talk
I had.

And I didn't even know
I was doing it.

So I made a decision—

To be intentional

about speaking positively
to myself.

And it wasn't easy.

It took time.

But little by little…

My thoughts changed.

And my mindset
began to shift.

One of the most powerful lessons
I learned was this—

Love yourself first.

I used to think…

If I loved others first…

they would love me back.

But that's not always
how it works.

You cannot make someone
love you.

But you can
love yourself.

And that realization…

was freeing.

When I began
to truly practice
self-love
and self-care…

I noticed a change.

In how I felt
about myself.

In how I showed up
in relationships.

In how I handled
situations in my life.

It didn't happen overnight.

It took time
to truly understand
what it meant

to love myself.

But now…

I walk in it.

I even encourage others
to do the same.

Because self-love
is not optional.

It is necessary.

For your mental health.
For your emotional health.
For your spiritual well-being.

And self-care…

is a part of that.

I had to learn
how to rest.

To slow down.

I used to work jobs
where I was constantly moving…

always on my feet.

And when I got home…

I would go straight to bed.

Then in 2022…

I got a customer service job.

A sit-down job.

And I thought—

"This will be easier."

But it wasn't.

I was more drained.

Because now…

I was dealing with people
all day.

Conversations.
Energy.
Emotions.

Customers were the hardest part.

And when I got home…

I had to decompress.

I had to unwind.

I had to reset.

Through rest.
Through prayer.
Through meditation.

So I could be ready
for the next day.

And that's when I realized—

Self-care
is not just physical.

It's emotional.

It's mental.

It's spiritual.

And it is necessary
to function
at your best.

Because at the end of the day…

Loving yourself
and taking care of yourself…

Is not selfish.

It's essential.

Resources – Self Love & Self Care

If you are on a journey
of learning how to love yourself…

Take your time.

Because self-love
is not something
that happens overnight.

It is learned.
It is practiced.
It is lived.

And you deserve
to experience it fully.

Learning Self-Love

- Watch content from
  Tonya TKO
  (Self-love, healing, and personal growth)
- Watch content from
  Andrea Lewis
  (Lifestyle, wellness, and self-care insights)

Daily Self-Love Practices

- Speak positively to yourself
- Look in the mirror and affirm yourself
- Celebrate small wins
- Give yourself grace when you fall short
- Set healthy boundaries

Self-Care Ideas

- Get proper rest and sleep
- Take quiet time to reset (no phone, no noise)
- Pray, meditate, or sit in stillness
- Eat for health, not just appearance
- Move your body in ways that feel good

Emotional & Mental Care

- Journal your thoughts and feelings
- Identify negative self-talk and replace it
- Take breaks when you feel overwhelmed
- Protect your peace and your energy

Body Acceptance

- Embrace your body as it is
- Focus on health over perfection
- Release unrealistic beauty standards
- Remember—your body is not the problem

A Final Reminder

You do not have to earn
your worth.

You do not have to prove
your value.

You are already enough.

And learning to love yourself…

Is one of the most powerful things
you will ever do.

The Love of Poetry Room

I have always loved poetry.

Even as a child…

English was my favorite subject
in school.

I loved reading.

Literature.
Stories.

Poetry

Especially Black literature.

Writers who told stories
that felt real.

That felt familiar.

Some of my favorite authors were
Nikki Giovanni,
Toni Morrison,
and Alice Walker.

But my favorite of them all…

was
Maya Angelou.

I admired her deeply.

Her voice.
Her strength.
Her storytelling.

Her words
carried power.

Years later…

poetry found me again.

During a breakup.

With someone
I thought I was going to marry.

But it didn't work out
that way.

And I needed an outlet.

I needed somewhere
to put the pain.

And that's when
I turned to poetry.

I began writing
about that situation.

About how I felt.

And in doing that…

I began to heal.

What started as pain…

turned into expression.

And after a while…

I realized—

I didn't have to only write

about heartbreak.

I could write
about anything.

My faith.
My thoughts.
My life.
The world around me.

That's when poetry
became more than just an outlet.

It became
a part of me.

I remember the first time
I ever performed
spoken word.

It was at a church event.

Pastor D invited me
to share a piece.

This was around 2011…

when I had relocated
back to Raleigh.

I was nervous.

So nervous.

But I did it anyway.

The first poem I ever performed
in front of an audience
was called—

"Keeping the Faith"
(Hebrews 11:1)

And when I finished…

The people received it.

They supported me.

They enjoyed it.

And in that moment…

Something clicked.

I had found
another part of myself.

One of the first spoken word artists
I ever listened to was

Janette Ikz.

I was introduced to her
by someone I was dating
at the time.

And when I heard her…

I was amazed.

Her delivery.
Her expression.
Her storytelling.

It was powerful.

One of the first poems
I heard from her was—

"I Will Wait for You."

A poem about love.
About patience.
About purpose.

It wasn't just about a man—

It was about
alignment.

And later…

when she got married…

She performed
"I Waited for You."

And seeing that…

Seeing the manifestation
of what she once spoke…

Was powerful.

It showed me
the power of words.

The power of speaking
what you believe.

In 2011…

I bought a composition notebook.

And I started writing.

About everything.

My feelings.
My thoughts.
My experiences.

And over time…

My voice developed.

Most of my poetry
centers around—

Faith.
God.
Love.
Life.
What's happening in the world.

And I love storytelling.

So I bring that
into my poetry.

Because every poem…

tells a story.

I used to go
to open mics.

And I loved it.

The energy.
The creativity.
The community.

But life happened.

Work.
Responsibilities.
Stability.

And I didn't always have the time
to fully dive into poetry
the way I wanted to.

But my love for it…

never left.

To this day…

when I want to tap into creativity…

I listen to
Maya Angelou.

Her poems like
"Still I Rise"
and *"Phenomenal Woman"*…

They ground me.

They remind me
of the power of words.

Of identity.
Of resilience.
Of voice.

And when I write…

I tap into that same spirit.

The Gift of Poetry

The beautiful gift of poetry…

Let us not take for granted
the gift
that has been given to us.

Poetry is like golden dust
falling from the sky…

Continuous.
Timeless.

It is as precious
as silver and gold.

A gift to the world.

Let us remember
those who came before us.

Those who paved the way.

Maya Angelou
who gave us *Phenomenal Woman*
and *Still I Rise*.

Nikki Giovanni
who gave us *Nikki-Rosa*.

Gwendolyn Brooks
who gave us *We Real Cool*.

Countee Cullen
whose words still echo today.

And so many more…

Their voices
live on through us.

Poetry is a gift—

Like a beautifully wrapped present
on Christmas morning.

Precious.
Intentional.
Meaningful.

From sonnets…
to haikus…
to spoken word…
to poetic prose…

Poetry is expression.

Poetry is healing.

Poetry is legacy.

So let us never forget…

The beautiful gift of poetry.

And let us continue…

to share it with the world.

The Love of Poetry Room – Healing Reflection (Expanded)

Healing in the Room – Vee Mayo

There are some things in life that don't just entertain you…
they *heal you.*

For me, poetry became that place.

Long before I even realized it, I had a love for words.
A love for expression.
A love for stories.

But it wasn't until I went through heartbreak…
until I felt something I didn't quite know how to explain…
that poetry became more than just something I liked.

It became an outlet.

A safe space.

A place where I could say what I didn't know how to say out loud.

When I picked up that pen and started writing,
I wasn't trying to be perfect.
I wasn't trying to impress anyone.

I was just trying to *release.*

Release the emotions.
Release the confusion.
Release the pain.

And somewhere in that process…
I began to heal.

What started as writing about one situation…
turned into something much bigger.

I realized I could write about life.
About faith.

About love.
About everyday experiences.

Poetry gave me permission to feel.

It gave me permission to be honest.

It gave me permission to be *me*.

And then came the moment where I had to step outside of my comfort zone…
and share it.

Standing in front of people for the first time,
I was nervous.

But there was something powerful about speaking what I had written.

Because it wasn't just words anymore…
it was my truth.

And I realized something in that moment:

My voice mattered.

Poetry taught me that my story had value.
That my perspective had meaning.
That my experiences could connect with someone else.

And even now, poetry remains a part of me.

It's not just something I do…
it's something that flows through me.

It's a gift.

A gift that connects me to myself…
and connects me to others.

Healing doesn't always look like therapy sessions or long conversations.

Sometimes…
healing looks like a pen, a page, and honesty.

Conclusion

As I reflect
over my life…

Over every chapter…
every room…
every season…

I see more
than just moments.

I see growth.

I see healing.

I see God's hand
in everything.

Even in the things
I didn't understand
at the time.

This journey…

has not been easy.

There were moments
of pain.

Moments of confusion.

Moments where I felt lost…
rejected…
alone.

But through it all…

I was never alone.

Every experience…

was shaping me.

Every setback…

was teaching me.

Every loss…

was preparing me.

And every room…

held a piece
of my healing.

From childhood…
to young adulthood…

From rejection…
to self-love…

From brokenness…
to wholeness…

I have come
a long way.

I have learned…

That healing
is a process.

That forgiveness
is a choice.

That self-love
is necessary.

And that faith…

is everything.

I've learned
that I cannot depend
on people
to fill voids
that only God can fill.

I've learned
that I am enough.

Not because
of what I have done…

But because
of who I am.

I've learned
to let go…

Of people.
Of places.
Of things…

That no longer serve me.

And I've learned
to embrace peace.

To choose growth.

To choose healing.

To choose me.

And most importantly…

I've learned
to choose God.

Because at the end of the day…

My relationship with God
has been the anchor
through it all.

When people left…
God remained.

When things didn't make sense…
God was still present.

When I felt like giving up…
God gave me strength.

And because of that…

I am still here.

Still standing.

Still growing.

Still becoming.

This is not the end
of my story.

It is only
the beginning.

Because healing…

does not stop here.

It continues.

And as I continue
on this journey…

I carry everything
I have learned.

And I use it…

to help others.

To encourage others.

To remind others…

That no matter
what you've been through…

You can heal.

You can grow.

You can become
everything
you were created to be.

And if you take
nothing else
from my story…

Take this—

Healing is possible.

And it can start
right where you are.

In your room.

— **Vee Mayo**

www.ingramcontent.com/pod-product-compliance
Lightning Source LLC
LaVergne TN
LVHW010611100826
845148LV00014B/2918

* 9 7 9 8 2 3 4 0 6 6 9 4 7 *